SUBJECT CATALOGING DIVISION
PROCESSING SERVICES
LIBRARY OF CONGRESS

CLASSIFICATION
CLASS P-PZ

Language and Literature Tables

LIBRARY OF CONGRESS
WASHINGTON 1982

The additions and changes in Class P-PZ adopted while
this work was in press will be cumulated and printed
in List 206 of **LC Classification—Additions
and Changes**

Library of Congress Cataloging in Publication Data

Library of Congress. Subject Cataloging Division.
  Classification—class P-PZ.

  "The additions and changes in class P-PZ adopted
while this work was in press will be cumulated and
printed in List 206 of LC classification—additions
and changes"—Verso t.p.
    Supt. of Docs. no.: LC 30.2:C56
    1. Classification—Books—Language and languages—
Tables.   2. Classification—Books—Literature—
Tables.   3. Classification, Library of Congress—
Tables.   I. Title.
Z696.U5P88   1982   025.4′33   81-23640
ISBN 0-8444-0389-χ   AACR2

For sale for $8 by the Cataloging Distribution Service,
Library of Congress, Washington, D.C. 20541. Subscribers
to the card service can charge purchases to their accounts;
others must pay in advance by check or money order payable
to the Chief, Cataloging Distribution Service, Library of
Congress. Payment from foreign countries may be made with
UNESCO coupons. Price includes postage.

PREFACE

Since the first schedules of Class P were issued, the Library of Congress has generally issued the tables used in each subclass as an appendix to the appropriate schedule. Exceptions to this practice were occasionally made, making it necessary to consult another schedule for the required tables. Seemingly identical tables were published in different schedules with minor variations. Changes made to these tables throughout the years have created further variations. In some cases tables were printed within the schedule, instead of in the appendix. The result of these practices has been confusion and inconsistency.

To reduce confusion and to promote more convenient and consistent changes, the Library is issuing all frequently-used tables of Class P in this one volume. All tables were examined and revised as necessary to eliminate unnecessary or undesirable variations. Similar tables were combined, some infrequently-used tables were cancelled, and one new table was created. Changes were made with consideration for a minimum amount of disruption to previously classified material. Some tables have been renumbered so that no two tables would be referred to by the same number.

Included in this publication is a conversion table showing the old and new numbering. The individual subclasses are being revised to reflect this new numbering. List 206 of *LC Classification—Additions and Changes* will show appropriate changes made throughout Class P, reflecting the new and/or changed table numbering. It will also show the cancellation of previously published tables.

Millicent Wewerka, subject cataloger in the humanities, is primarily responsible for the content of this publication. The editorial work was done by Lawrence Buzard, editor of classification.

Mary K. D. Pietris
Chief, Subject Cataloging Division

Joseph H. Howard
Assistant Librarian for Processing
Services

CONVERSION TABLES

The following tables show the old table numbers used in
the Class P classification schedules and the corresponding
new numbers. In some cases there are no changes.

LANGUAGE TABLES

Old number	New number
I	I
II	II
III	III
IV	IV
V	V
VI	VI
VIa	VI
VII	IX xxV ?
VIII	VIII
VIIIa	VIIIa
IX	IX
X	Cancelled
XI	XI
XIa	XI
XII	XII
XIII	IX
XIV	XIV
XV	XV
XVa	XVa
XVb	XV
XVI	XVI

CONVERSION TABLES

LITERATURE TABLES

Old number	New number
V (PT, Part 2)	XXIX
XX	Cancelled
XXI	Cancelled
XXII	XXII
XXIII	XXIII
XXIV	XXIV
XXV	XXV
XXVI	Cancelled
XXVIa	Cancelled
XXVII	XXIV
XXVIII	XXIV
XXIX	XXIX
XXIXa	Cancelled
XXX	XXX
XXXa	XXX
A	XX
B	Cancelled
C	Cancelled
D	XXIII
Da	XXIII
Da (PR)	XXI
E	XXIV
Ea	XXIV
F	XXVI
Fa	XXV

CONVERSION TABLES

INDIVIDUAL AUTHORS AND WORKS

Old number	New number
I	Cancelled
II	XXXI
III	XXXII
IIIa	XXXII
IV	XXXIII
IVa	XXXIII
V	Cancelled
VI	XXXIV
VII	XXXV
VIII	XXXVII
VIIIa	XXXIX
VIIIb	XXXIX
IX	XXXVIII
IXa	XL
IXb	XL
X	XLI
Xa	XLi
XI	XLIII
XII	XXXVI
XIIa	Cancelled
XIII	XXVIII
XIIIa	Cancelled
XXXI	XLIV
XXXII	XXXIX

CONVERSION TABLES

INDIVIDUAL AUTHORS AND WORKS

Old number	New number
XXXIIa	XL
XXXIII	XLI
XXXIIIa	XLI
XXXIV	XLIII

LANGUAGE

TABLES OF SUBDIVISIONS

	I (900)	II (500)	III (200)	IV (100)	V (50)
Periodicals. Serials					
International	1.A1-3				
English and American	1.A4-Z	1			
French	2		1		
German	3				
Other (not A-Z)	9	3		1	1
Annuals. Yearbooks, etc.	10	4			
Societies	11-19	5-7	3		
Subarranged like Periodicals					
Congresses	21	9			
Collections (nonserial)				2	2
Texts, sources, etc.	23	11	5		
Class here only collections of texts					
For texts and studies, see Table I, 25, etc.					
For readers, see Table I, 117, etc.					
Monographs. Studies	25	13	7		
Studies in honor of a particular person or institution, A-Z	26	14	8		
Individual authors	27	15	9		
Encyclopedias	31	19	11	3	3
Atlases, maps, charts, tables, etc.	33	20	12	4	
Prefer Table I, 777, etc.					
Philosophy. Theory. Method ...	35	21	13	5	4
Relations	37	23			
History of philology					
Cf. Table I, 65-69, etc., Study and teaching Table I, 75-87, etc., History of the language					
General works	51	25	15	7	5
General special	52	26			
By period					
Earliest	53				
Middle Ages	54	27			
Renaissance	55				
Modern	57	29			
19th-20th centuries	58				
By region or country, A-Z	60	31			
Biography, memoirs, etc.					
Collective	63	33	17.A2	9.A2	6.A2
Individual, A-Z	64	34	.A5-Z	.A5-Z	.A5-Z

LANGUAGE

TABLES OF SUBDIVISIONS

	I (900)	II (500)	III (200)	IV (100)	V (50)
Study and teaching. Research					
General works	65	35	19	11	7
General special	66	36			
By period, see Table I, 53-58, 75-87, etc.					
By region or country, A-Z	68	38	20		
By school, A-Z	69	39	21		
By research institute, A-Z	.5	.5	.5		
General works					
Early to 1800	70	40	22		
Treatises (Philology, General)	71	41	23	} 13	} 8
General special	73	43	.5	14	
Relation to other languages .	74	44	24		
Language data processing	.5	.5	.5		
Language standardization and variation	.7	.7	.7		
Spoken language	.8	.8	.8		
History of the language					
General works	75	45	25	15	9
Early, see Table I, 53, etc.					
Middle Ages	77				
(15th)-16th century	79	} 47			
(16th)-17th century	81				
(17th)-18th century	83	} 49			
19th century	85				
20th century	87	} 51			
By region, see Dialects, Table I, 700-840, etc.					
Outlines	93	55	26	16	.5
Popular	95	57	27	17	10
Script	97	58	28	.5	.5
Grammar					
Comparative (Two or more languages)	99	59	29	18	} 11
Historical	101	61	31	19	
General works			33	21	
To 1800	103	63			
1800-	105	64			
General special	107	65	34	22	12
Textbooks			35	23	13
History and criticism	108	.5	.A2	.A2	.A2
Early to 1870	109	66	}		
1870-1949	111	67	.A3-Z	.A3-Z	.A3-Z
1950-	112	.3			

2

LANGUAGE

TABLES OF SUBDIVISIONS

	I (900)	II (500)	III (200)	IV (100)	V (50)
Grammar – Continued					
Self-instructors	112.5	67.5	35.5	23.5	
Audiovisual instructors	.7	.7	.7	.7	
Readers					
History and criticism	.9	.9	.9	.9	
Series	113	68	36	24	
Primers. Primary grade					
readers	115	69	} 37		
Intermediate and advanced ..	117	71		25	
Outlines, syllabi, tables,					
etc.	118	.3	.3	.3	
Examination questions, etc. ..	119	.5	.5	.5	
Manuals for special classes					
of students, A–Z	120	72	38	26	

.C6   Commercial
           Cf. HF5719, Business
                report writing
           HF5721, Business
                correspondence
.G35   Gardeners
.M3   Medical personnel

.P64   Police
.R4   Restaurant personnel

       Self-instructors, see
          Table I, 112.5, etc.

.S45   Servants
.S57   Social workers
.T42   Technical

	I (900)	II (500)	III (200)	IV (100)	V (50)
Conversation. Phrase books ...	121	73	39	27	
Plays for acting in schools					
and colleges	123	74			
Idioms, errors, etc., see					
Table I, 460, etc.					
Readers on special					
subjects, A–Z	127	.2	.15	.15	

.A45   Africa
.A46   Africa, North

.A7   Art
.B5   Biography

.C5   Civilization
.C6   Commerce

LANGUAGE

TABLES OF SUBDIVISIONS

	I (900)	II (500)	III (200)	IV (100)	V (50)
Grammar					
Readers on special subjects, A-Z - Cont.	127	74.2	39.15	27.15	
.C8 Current events					
.D48 Detective and mystery stories					
.D7 Drama					
.E25 Economics					
.F35 Fantastic fiction					
.F7 France					
.G4 Geography					
.H5 History					
.L34 Latin America					
.L4 Legends					
Literature, see Table I, 113-117, etc.					
.M3 Mathematics					
.M38 Medicine					
.M39 Mexican-Americans					
.M4 Mexico					
.M48 Military art and science					
.M5 Minorities					
Mystery stories, see .D48					
.M87 Music					
.N27 National characteristics					
.N3 Naval science					
.N48 New Mexico					
.P45 Philosophy					
.P63 Poetry					
.P64 Poland					
.R34 Railroads					
.R86 Russian history					
.S4 Science					
.S6 Social sciences					
.S63 Spain					
.T47 Theater					
Travels, see .V68					
.V68 Voyages and travels					

LANGUAGE

TABLES OF SUBDIVISIONS

	I (900)	II (500)	III (200)	IV (100)	V (50)
Grammar – Continued					
Textbooks for foreign students (other than English)					
Theory, methods, etc., for teachers	127.8	74.3	39.2	27.2	
General	128	.5	.3	.3	
By nationality, A–Z	129	75	.5	.5	
Phonology	131	76	40	28	15
Including phonemics Cf. Table I, 153–165, etc., Alphabet					
Phonetics	135	77	41	29	
Pronunciation	137	79	43	31	
Accent	139	81	44	32	
Clitics	.3	.3	.3	.3	
Intonation	.5	.5	.5	.5	
Prosodic analysis	.7	.7	.7	.7	
Phonetics of the sentence (Sandhi)	140	82	.9	.9	
Orthography. Spelling					17
History	141	} 83	45	33	
General works	143				
Spelling books		85	47	35	
To 1860	144				
1860–					
Rules	145				
List of words	146				
Spelling reform		87	49		
Associations, collections, etc.	149				
To ca. 1870	150				
1870–	151				
Phonetic readers	152	88	50	36	
Alphabet	153	89	51	37	18
Transliteration	154	90	52		
Vowels	155	91	53		
Diphthongs	157	92	54		
Consonants	159	93	55		
Contraction (Hiatis. Elision)	161	94	56		
Particular letters	165	97	57		
Syllabication	168	98	58		
Punctuation, see Table I, 450, etc.					
Capitalization	169	99	.5		
Morphophonemics	170	100	.9	38	.9

LANGUAGE

TABLES OF SUBDIVISIONS

	I (900)	II (500)	III (200)	IV (100)	V (50)
Grammar - Continued					
Morphology	171	101	59	39	19
Word formation	175	103	61	40	
Inflection					
General works	180	104	62	41	
Noun. Declension 1/	(181)	(105)	(63)	(42)	
Adjective. Adverb.					
Comparison 1/	(186)	(107)	(65)	(43)	
Verb. Conjugation 1/ ...	(196)	(109)	(67)	(45)	
Tables. Paradigms	197	111	69	47	
Parts of speech (Morphology and Syntax)					
General works	199	119	70	48	21
Noun					
General works	201	121	71	49	
General special	205	123			
Gender	211	125	} 73		
Number	216	127			
Case	221	129	75		
Adjective. Adverb.					
Comparison	241	133	77	53	
Numerals	246	135	79	55	
Article	251	137	81	57	
Pronoun	261	141	83	59	
Verb	271	145	85	61	
Person	276	147	87		
Number	280	149	88		
Voice	285	151	89		
Mood	290	153	91	} 64	
Tense	301	159	95		
Aspects of verbal action	306	160	.5		
Infinitive and participle	311	162	96		
Participle, gerund, etc.	312	164			
Special classes of verbs, A-Z	315	165	97	65	
.A8 Auxiliary					
.F3 Factitive					
.I46 Imperative					
.I6 Impersonal					
.I8 Irregular					
.P52 Phrasal					
.P4 Periphrastic					
.R4 Reflexive					

1/

  Prefer "Parts of speech ..." in Table I, 199+, etc.

LANGUAGE

TABLES OF SUBDIVISIONS

	I (900)	II (500)	III (200)	IV (100)	V (50)
Grammar					
Verb – Continued					
Particular verbs, A-Z	317	167	98	66	
Other. Miscellaneous	318	169	99	.5	
Particle	321	171	101	67	
Adverb	325	173	103		
Preposition	335	177	105		
Postposition	340	179	106		
Conjunction	345	181	107		
Interjection	355	187	109		
Other special, A-Z	359	191	111		
.N4 Negatives					
Syntax				71	23
General works	361	201	113		
Outlines	365	205	115		
General special	369	207	117		
Sentences					
General arrangement, etc.	375	211	119		
Order of words	380	213	121		
Order of clauses	385	215	123		
Clauses	390	217	125		
Other special	395	225	127		
Grammatical usage of particu-					
lar authors, A-Z	400	231	131	73	26
Prefer PA, PQ – PT					
Style. Composition.					
Rhetoric				75	27
General works	410	240	135		
Textbooks	420	245	137		
Outlines, questions, exer-					
cises and specimens. List					
of subjects	430	250	139		
Special authors, A-Z	433	251	140		
Prefer PA, PQ – PT					
Discourse analysis	434	252	.5		
Special parts of rhetoric ...			141		
Style. Invention, narra-					
tion, etc.	435	253			
Other special. Figures,					
tropes, allegory, etc. ..	440	255			
Choice of words. Vocabu-					
lary, etc.	445	256	142		
Punctuation	450	258	143		
Idioms. Errors.					
Blunders	460	260	145	79	

LANGUAGE

TABLES OF SUBDIVISIONS

	I (900)	II (500)	III (200)	IV (100)	V (50)
Style. Composition.					
Rhetoric – Continued					
Special classes of composition					
Essays	471				
Lectures	473				
Newspaper style	474	263	147		
Scientific papers	475				
Precis writing	477				
Report writing	478				
Other, A–Z	479				
.P6 Political literature					
Letter writing		265	149	80	
Early to 1800	481				
1800–	483				
Business, see HF					
Diplomatic, see JX					
Etiquette, see BJ					
Love letters, see HQ					
Textbooks	485				
Specimens. Collections ..		267	.5		
Early to 1850/1870	495				
1850/1870–	497				
Translating	498	268	150	.5	28
For special subjects, see					
B – Z, e. g. T11.5, Tech-					
nology					
Machine translating	499	269	.5		
Including research					
Prosody. Metrics. Rhythmics ..				81	29
History of the science	501	271	151		
General works					
Early to 1800	504	274	152		
1800–	505	275	153		
Textbooks	509	279	155		
Versification (Gradus ad Par-					
nassum)	511	281	157		
Rhyme	517	283	158		
Rhyming dictionaries	519				
Special. By form, A–Z	521	285			
e. g. .E6 Epic					
.L9 Lyric					
Special meters, A–Z	531	290			
.A3 Alexandrine					
.D4 Decasyllable					
.F8 Free verse					
Other special	541	295	159		
e. g. Epithets					
Cf. Table I, 440, etc.					

LANGUAGE

TABLES OF SUBDIVISIONS

	I (900)	II (500)	III (200)	IV (100)	V (50)
Prosody. Metrics.					
Rhythmics - Continued					
Special authors, see author					
or work, e. g. PR3085,					
Shakespeare	(551)	(297)			
Rhythm	559	298	} 160		
Rhythm in prose	561	299			
Lexicology	567	.5	.5	82	30
Etymology					
Treatises	571	301	161	83	31
Popular works	574	302	.5		
Names (General)	576	303	162	.3	
Cf. CS2300+, Personal names					
DA645, DB15, G104,					
etc., Place names					
Dictionaries (exclusively					
etymological	580	305	163	.5	
Special elements. By language,					
A-Z	582	307	164	84	
.A3 Foreign elements					
(General)					
Cf. Table I, 670, etc.,					
Dictionaries					
Other special	583	.5	.3	.3	
Folk etymology	584	308	.5	.5	
Semantics	585	310	165	85	32
Symonyms. Antonyms	591				
Paronyms	593	} 315	167	86	33
Homonyms	595				
Particular words, A-Z	599	319	169	.9	.9
Lexicography					
Periodicals. Societies. Serials					
Collections (nonserial)	601	320	171		
General works	611	323	173	} 87	34
Biography of lexicographers,					
see Table I, 63-64, etc.					
Criticism, etc., of particular					
dictionaries	617	.5	.5		
Dictionaries					
Dictionaries with definitions					
in same language			175	89	35
Early to 1800	620	325			
1800-	625	327			
Minor, abridged, school					
dictionaries	628				
Picture dictionaries	629	328	176		
Supplementary dictionaries.					
Dictionaries of new words	630	329	177		

LANGUAGE

TABLES OF SUBDIVISIONS

	I (900)	II (500)	III (200)	IV (100)	V (50)
Lexicography					
Dictionaries – Continued					
Dictionaries with definitions in two or more languages, or dictionaries of two or more languages with definitions in one language ..	635	331	178	90	36
Dictionaries with definitions in English	640	333	179	91	
Dictionaries with definitions in other languages, A–Z	645	335	181	93	37
Dictionaries exclusively etymological, see Table I, 580, etc.					
Dictionaries of particular periods (other than periods separately specified elsewhere)	650	337	182	.2	38
Dictionaries of particular authors, see the author in PA – PT	(655)	(339)			
Dictionaries of names	660	341	183		
Cf. Table I, 673, etc., Foreign words CS, Genealogy					
Dictionaries, etc. of obsolete, archaic words and provincialisms	667	342	185		
Local provincialisms, see Dialects					
Dictionaries of foreign words					
General	670	343	184	95	39
Names	673	344			
Special. By language, see Table I, 582, etc.					
Other special lists			185		
Glossaries	680	345			
By subject, A–Z (added entry only)	(683)	(346)			
Classified in A – N, Q – Z					
Dictionaries of terms and phrases	689	347			

LANGUAGE

TABLES OF SUBDIVISIONS

	I (900)	II (500)	III (200)	IV (100)	V (50)
Lexicography					
Dictionaries					
Other special lists - Cont.					
Word frequency lists	691	348			
Cf. Table I, 445, etc., Vocabulary, etc.					
For research on word frequency, etc., in connection with machine translating, see Table I, 499, etc.			185	95	39
Reverse indexes	692	.5			
Abbreviations, List of ...	693	349			
Linguistic geography. Dialects, etc. 1/					
Linguistic geography	700	350	187.A1	96.A1	41.A1
Cf. Table I, 777, etc., Atlases					
Dialects, provincialisms, etc.					
For language standardization and variation, see Table I, 74.7, etc.					
Periodicals. Collections ..	701	351	.A2-29	.A2-29	.A2-29
Collections of texts, etc. .	707	353	.A3-Z	.A3	.A3
General works	710	355	188		
Grammar	720	361	189	.A5-Z	.A5-Z
Phonology. Phonetics	725	365			
Morphology	735	370			
Syntax	750	375			
Other	760	380			
Dictionaries	770	390	191	97	43
Atlases, maps, charts, tables	777	393	192	98.A1 By date	45.A1 By date
Local. By region, place, etc., A-Z	780	395	193	.A5-Z 99	.A5-Z 46
Slang. Argot					
Collections	800	400	195		
General works	810	407	196		
Dictionaries. Lists	815	411	197		
Texts	820	416	.5		

1/
   For nearly all of the more important languages spoken in Europe special schemes for dialects have been made; see PC787+, PC1701+, etc.

LANGUAGE

TABLES OF SUBDIVISIONS

	I (900)	II (500)	III (200)	IV (100)	V (50)
Linguistic geography. Dialects, etc. 1/ Slang. Argot - Continued Special topics, A-Z	830	421	198		
.B88 Butchers' language .C35 Cant .C6 Court and courtiers language .P6 Political language .R3 Railroad language .S66 Sports language .W65 Women's language .W67 World War II					
Special local, A-Z	840	431	199		

1/
    For nearly all of the more important languages spoken in Europe special schemes
for dialects have been made; see PC787+, PC1701+, etc.

LANGUAGE

TABLES OF SUBDIVISIONS

TABLE VI

1	Periodicals. Societies. Serials. Collections (nonserial)
2	Congresses
3	History of philology
5	Study and teaching
6	General works
7	History of the language
8	Script
	Grammar
9	General works
11	Phonology
12	Transliteration
13	Morphology
14	Parts of speech
15	Syntax
17	Style. Composition. Rhetoric
18	Translating
19	Prosody. Metrics. Rhythmics
20	Lexicology
21	Etymology
	Lexicography
23	Dictionaries with definitions in the same language
25	Dictionaries with definitions in English and other languages
26	Lists of words
	Dialects
27	General works
28A–Z	Special. By name or place, A–Z
29	Slang. Argot

TABLE VIII

1	General works
2	Grammar
5	Etymology. Lexicography. Dictionaries
7	Miscellaneous
9	Texts and commentaries

TABLE VIIIa

1.A1–5	Periodicals. Societies. Serials. Collections (nonserial)
.A6–Z	General works
2	General special (Script)
	Grammar. Treatises. Textbooks
3	Western
4	Oriental and other non-Western
5	Exercises. Readers. Phrase books, etc.
	Dictionaries
6	Western
7	Oriental and other non-Western
8	Literature (XXV)
9	Other special
	e. g. Etymology

LANGUAGE

TABLES OF SUBDIVISIONS

TABLE IX

1	Periodicals. Societies. Serials. Collections (nonserial)
2	General works
3	Grammar
4	Dictionaries
5	Texts

TABLE XI

	Language
1	General works
2	Grammar
3	Dictionaries
	Literature
.5	History
4.A2A-Z	Collections 1/
.A3-Z5	Individual authors or works, A-Z (XL or XLIII) 1/
.Z9A-Z	Local. By dialect name or place, A-Z
	For language groups use local number for works too general to be classed with an individual language or separately classed smaller group
.Z95A-Z	Translations into foreign languages, A-Z
	Subarranged by date

1/
   For language groups use 4.A2-Z5 for collections and omit numbers for individual authors

---

TABLE XII

1	Periodicals. Societies. Serials. Collections (nonserial)
2	General works
3	General special
4	Grammar
5	Metrics
6	Etymology. Lexicography. Dictionaries
7A-Z	Local. By dialect name or place, A-Z
	For language groups use local number for works too general to be classed with an individual language or separately classed smaller group
8	Texts

LANGUAGE

TABLES OF SUBDIVISIONS

	XIV	XV
Periodicals. Societies. Serials.		
Collections (nonserial)	1.A1-5	.A1-5
General works. Grammar	.A6-Z	.A6-Z3
Dictionaries	2	.Z5
Texts	3	.Z77
Local. By dialect name or place, A-Z	4.A-Z9	.Z9A-Z
For language groups use local number for works too general to be classed with an individual language or separately classed smaller group		
Translations into foreign languages, A-Z .	.Z95A-Z	.Z95A-Z
Subarranged by date		

	XVa (one number) 1/	XVI (Cutter number) 1/
Language		
General works	x	.x
Grammar	.1	.x1
Exercises. Readers. Phrase books, etc.	.2	.x2
Etymology	.3	.x3
Dictionaries	.4	.x4
Literature		
History	.5	.x5
Collections		
Including translations		
General	.6	.x6
Poetry	.7	.x7
Folk literature	.8	.x8
Individual authors or works, A-Z	.9A-Z	.x9A-Z
Subarrange Table XVa by Tables XL or XLIII		
Dialects		
General works	.94	.x94
Special. By name or place, A-Z	.95A-Z	.x95A-Z

1/
    x=Integer or Cutter number. Substitute the language or dialect and
literature for x in the Table, e. g. PC4813.7, Ladino poetry; PL65.K57,
Kirghiz poetry

LITERATURE

TABLES OF SUBDIVISIONS

	XX	XXI
History and criticism		
Periodicals. Societies. Serials		0
Periodicals	0	
Yearbooks	1	
Societies	2	
Congresses	3	
Museums. Exhibitions	.5	
Collected works (nonserial)		
Several authors	4	
Individual authors	5	.1
Encyclopedias. Dictionaries	6	.2
Study and teaching		
General works	8	2.2
Individual schools. By name, A-Z	9	.3
Biography of scholars, teachers, etc.		
Collective	.4	.7
Individual, A-Z	.5	3
History		
General works		
Early works	10	4.2
Modern treatises	11	.3
Textbooks	12	.4
Outlines, syllabi, quizzes, etc.	13	.5
Addresses, essays, lectures	14	.6
Awards, prizes (not A-Z)	17	.8
Relation to history, civilization,		
culture, etc.	18	5.2
Relation to other literatures	19	.3
Translations (as a subject)	20	.4
Foreign authors (General)	21	.45
Treatment of special subjects, classes, etc.		
Subjects, A-Z	22	.5
.A37 Adventure		
.C7 Crime		
.F76 Frontier and pioneer life		
.M6 Modernism		
.N3 Nature		
.R4 Religion		
.S6 Social problems		
.T3 Tango (Dance)		
.W45 The West		

LITERATURE

TABLES OF SUBDIVISIONS

	XX	XXI
History and criticism		
History		
Treatment of special subjects, classes,		
etc. – Continued		
Classes, A-Z	23	5.6
.A1 Characters (General)		
.A88 Australian aborigines		
.G3 Gauchos		
.I45 Immigrants		
.I5 Indians, American		
.J4 Jews		
.P7 Priests		
.W6 Women		
Individual characters, A-Z	25	.7
Biography		
Collective	27	6.2
By period, see special period below		
Individual, see 196+, 19+		
Memoirs, letters, etc.	29	.3
Literary landmarks. Homes and haunts of authors .	31	7
Women authors. Literary relations of women	33	8
Other classes of authors, A-Z	34	.2
.J48 Jewish		
By period		
Origins	35	⎫ 9
Medieval	38-40	⎬
Modern Under each:		
Renaissance .... (1) General works	44-46	.3
16th-18th century .. (2) Addresses, essays,	47-49	.4
lectures		
19th century .... (3) Special subjects	50-52	.5
20th century .... (not A-Z)	53-55	.6
Poetry		
History		
General works	61	10.2
Medieval, see 38-40, 9		
Modern		
16th-18th century	67	.3
(18th and) 19th century	69	.4
20th century	71	.5
Special forms or subjects		
Epic	77	.6
Lyric	79	.7
Popular poetry. Ballads, etc.	80	.8
Other, A-Z	81	.9

LITERATURE

TABLES OF SUBDIVISIONS

	XX	XXI
History and criticism - Continued		
Drama		
History		
General works	83	11.2
Early to 1800	85	.3
19th century	87	.4
20th century	89	.5
Special forms, A-Z	93	.6
.F6 Folk drama		
Special subjects, A-Z	95	.7
.S9 Symbolism		
Prose. Fiction		
History		
General works	97	12.2
Early to 1800	99	.3
19th century	101	.4
20th century	103	.5
Special topics, A-Z	107	.6

    .A39 Adventure
    .C45 Children's stories
    .C58 Cities and towns

    .D4 Death
    .E95 Existentialism
    .F27 Fantastic fiction
    .F4 Feuilletons

    .G74 Grotesque
    .H5 Historical fiction
    .I5 Immigrants
    .I54 Indians, American

    .I7 Ireland
    .I83 Italians

    .P7 Prairies
    .S26 Santiago de Chile
    .S34 Science fiction
    .S49 Sex

    .S6 Social classes
    .S8 Supernatural

    .U86 Utopias
    .W6 Women

LITERATURE

TABLES OF SUBDIVISIONS

	XX	XXI
History and criticism - Continued		
Other forms		
Oratory	109	13.2
Diaries	110	.3
Letters	111	.4
Essays	113	.5
Wit and humor	115	.6
Miscellaneous	117	.7
Folk literature	121	.8
Collections		
Periodicals	130	14
Comprehensive collections	133	.3
Selections. Anthologies	135	.4
Special classes of authors, A-Z	136	.5
.A47 Air pilots		
.B55 Blacks		
.C5 Children		
.C6 College students		
.E84 Eskimos		
.I5 Indians, American		
.M46 Mentally ill		
.P48 Physicians		
.P7 Prisoners		
.S3 School children		
.W6 Women		
Special topics, A-Z	.5	.52
.C3 Canada		
.C55 City and town life		
.F35 Family		
.F36 Fantasy		
.F57 Fire		
.F73 French-Canadians		
.F75 Frontier and pioneer life		
.G73 Grandmothers		
.I45 Immigration		
.L35 Landscape		
.P7 Prairies		
.S67 Spring		
.W38 Water		
.W66 Women		
Translations. By language, A-Z	137	.55

LITERATURE

TABLES OF SUBDIVISIONS

	XX	XXI
Collections - Continued		
By period		
Medieval	140	14.6
16th–18th centuries	141	.7
19th century	143	.8
20th century	144	.9
Local, see 191–192, 18.2+		
Poetry		
Periodicals	148	15.1
Comprehensive collections	150	.23
Selections. Anthologies	151	.25
Special classes of authors		
Women	153	.3
Other, A–Z	154	.35
.A8 Asians		
.B55 Blacks		
.C5 Children		
.C6 College students. College verse		
.I53 Indians, American		
.I8 Italians		
.P7 Prisoners		
.S3 Students. School verse		
By period		
Medieval	155	.4
15th–18th century	156	.5
19th century	157	.6
20th century	158	.7
Special. By form or subject		
Popular poetry. Ballads, etc.	160	.8
Cf. 189, 17.95, Folk literature		
Other, A–Z	161	.85
.A5 Anchieta, Jose de, 1534–1597		
.B8 Buenos Aires		
.C18 Canada		
.C35 Christian poetry		
.C4 Christmas		
College verse, see 154.C6, 15.35.C6		
.C64 Concrete poetry		
.D35 Death		
.D4 Descriptive poetry		
.D72 Drug abuse		
.E5 Elegaic poetry		
.E52 England		

LITERATURE

TABLES OF SUBDIVISIONS

	XX	XXI

Collections
  Poetry
    Special. By form or subject
    Other, A-Z - Continued ....
	161	15.85

.E75 Erotic poetry		
.F6 Fortaleza, Brazil		
.G3 Gauchos		
.H25 Haiku		
.H4 Heart		
.H5 History		
.H57 Honor		
.I53 Indians, American		
.I74 Irigoyen, Hipólito		
.J3 Jacobites		
.L3 Labor and laboring classes		
.L6 Love		
.L8 Lyrics. Songs		
.M18 Maclean, John, 1879-1923		
.M64 Mothers		
.N2 Narrative poetry		
.N64 Nonsense verse		
.O75 Orizaba, Mexico		
.P59 Political poetry		
.P7 Prison life		
.P76 Protest poetry		
.Q3 Quatrains		
.R3 Railroads		
.R39 Recife, Brazil		
.R4 Religious poetry		
.R59 Rizal y Alonso, Jose		
.S3 Satire		
.S4 Sea poetry		
.S57 Sonnets		
.S6 Spring		
.T3 Tango (Dance)		
.T7 Trees		
.V45 Vera Cruz, Mexico		
.W37 War		
.W45 Whales		

LITERATURE

TABLES OF SUBDIVISIONS

	XX	XI
Collections		
Poetry – Continued		
Translations. By language, A–Z	163	15.9
Drama		
Comprehensive collections	164	16.2
Selections. Anthologies	165	.3
Stories, plots, etc.	.5	.35
By period		
To 1800	166	.4
19th century	167	.5
20th century	169	.6
Special (Tragedies, comedies, etc.), A–Z	170	.7
.C48 Children's plays		
.O5 One-act plays		
.P3 Pastoral drama		
Translations. By language, A–Z	171	.8
Prose		
General prose collections	173	17.25
Fiction		
General collections	175	.3
Short stories	176	.32
Special classes of authors, A–Z	.2	.33
.J49 Jews		
.W65 Women		
Digests, synopses, etc.	.3	.34
Special. By form or subject, A–Z	.5	.35
Translations. By language, A–Z	177	.36
Oratory	179	.4
Diaries	180	.5
Letters	181	.6
Essays	183	.7
Wit and humor	185	.8
Miscellany	187	.9
Translations. By language, A–Z	188	.92
Folk literature	189	.95
Cf. 160, 15.8, Popular poetry, etc.		
Local		
By region, province, county, etc., A–Z (XXVI) ...	191	18.2
By city, A–Z (XXVI)	192	.3
Foreign countries, A–Z (XXVI)	193	.4
Individual authors, A–Z		
Each author is subarranged by Table XL, unless		
otherwise specified		
To 1810/25	196	19
1810/25–1960	197	.2
1961–	198–198.36	.3
For Table XX, further subarrange by XXIX		

LITERATURE

TABLES OF SUBDIVISIONS

TABLE XXII

	History and criticism
	Periodicals. Societies. Serials
	Collected works (nonserial)
1	Several authors
	Individual authors
2	Encyclopedias. Dictionaries
3	Study and teaching
	Biography of critics, historians, etc.
4	Collective
.5	Individual, A–Z
	History
5	General works
6	Addresses, essays, lectures
7	Relation to history, civilization, culture, etc.
8	Relation to other literatures
9	Translations (as subject)
10	Treatment of special subjects, classes, etc., A–Z

.L6	Love
.P68	Poverty
.P7	Psychology
.R4	Religion
.S4	Sex

13	Biography (Collected)
	By period
15	Origins
16	Modern
	Poetry
17	General works
	By period
18	To 1900
19	20th century
20	Special forms and topics (not A–Z)
21	Drama
23	Prose. Fiction
	Other forms
	Oratory
25	Letters
	Essays
27	Wit and humor
28	Miscellaneous
29	Folk literature
	Local, see 47
	Collections
31	Comprehensive collections
32	Selections. Anthologies

LITERATURE

TABLES OF SUBDIVISIONS

TABLE XXII

	Collections – Continued
32.5	Special classes of authors, A–Z
	.P6 Policemen
	.S6 Soldiers
	Poetry
34	General
35	Special forms and topics (not A–Z)
37	Drama
	Prose
39	General
40	Fiction
41	Oratory
42	Letters
43	Essays
44	Wit and humor
45	Miscellany
46	Folk literature
47	Local, A–Z (XXVI)
48	Individual authors, A–Z
	Each author subarranged by Table XL, unless otherwise specified

LITERATURE

TABLES OF SUBDIVISIONS

	XXIII	XXIV	XXV
History			
Periodicals. Societies. Serials	0	0.A1-5	0.A1-5
Congresses	.15	.A515	.A515
Encyclopedias. Dictionaries	.2	.A52	.A52
Study and teaching	.3	.A53	.A53
Biography of critics, historians,			
etc., A-Z	.6	.A56	.A56
General works	1	.A6-Z	.A6-Z
General special	2	.5	.05
Addresses, essays, lectures	3		
Biography (Collective)	4	1	.1
Origins	5		
To 1800	6		
19th century	7		
20th century	8		
Poetry	10	2	.2
Drama	11	3	.3
Other	12	4	.4
Collections			
Periodicals	.5	.5	.45
General	13	5	.5
Translations. By language, A-Z	.5	.5	.55
Poetry	14	6	.6
Translations. By language, A-Z	.5	.5	.65
Drama	15	7	.7
Other	16	8	.8
Local, A-Z (XXVI)	17	.5	.85
Individual authors or works, A-Z	19	9	.9
Each author or work subarranged by			
Table XL or XLIII, unless otherwise			
specified			

TABLE XXVI (x=Cutter number)

  .x   History
  .x2 Collections

LITERATURE

TABLES OF SUBDIVISIONS

TABLE XXVIII

Anonymous works in fiction, poetry, drama, etc.

Special number for anonymous works	Works by unidentified authors are to be classed under the period to which they belong and are to precede the works of individual authors known by name, except as otherwise provided for in the schedules
.A1	Works without any indication of author, either by symbol or initial. By title, A-Z
.A2	Works by authors indicated by non-alphabetic symbols (dots, dashes, asterisks, etc.). By title, A-Z
.A6	Works by authors indicated by a descriptive phrase. By first word of phrase, A-Z
	e. g. PQ2149.A6I5 (Un) Ingenieur en chef honoraire des mines
.A7	Works "By the author of" arranged by the title named
	e. g. PT1799.A7R8+ By the author or "Ruinen aus den sagen des nordens"

LITERATURE

TABLES OF SUBDIVISIONS

TABLE XXVIII

Anonymous works in fiction, poetry, drama, etc. - Continued

.A9	Works by A, A***, A - , Capt. A, etc. Subarranged in one alphabet by title disregarding symbols and other initials that may be added. The letters A, B, C, etc., in this and following captions represent a single initial or the supposed surname initial
.B3	Works by B
.C3	Works by C
.D3	Works by D
.E3	Works by E
.F3	Works by F
.G3	Works by G
.H3	Works by H
.I3	Works by I
.J3	Works by J
.K3	Works by K
.L3	Works by L
.M3	Works by M
.N3	Works by N
.O3	Works by O
.P3	Works by P
.Q3	Works by Q
.R3	Works by R
.S3	Works by S
.T3	Works by T
.U3	Works by U
.V3	Works by V
.W3	Works by W
.X3	Works by X
.Y3	Works by Y
.Z3	Works by Z

LITERATURE

TABLES OF SUBDIVISIONS

TABLE XXIX

The author number is determined by the second
  letter of the name
Each author is subarranged by Table XL, unless
  otherwise specified

0	Anonymous works. By title, A–Z
.1	A
.12	B
.13	C
.14	D
.15	E
.16	F
.17	G
.18	H
.19	I
.2	J
.21	K
.22	L
.23	M
.24	N
.25	O
.26	P
.27	Q
.28	R
.29	S
.3	T
.31	U
.32	V
.33	W
.34	X
.35	Y
.36	Z

LITERATURE

TABLES OF SUBDIVISIONS

TABLE XXX

	Translations into foreign languages
	Polyglot. Translations into several languages
(1).A1	General
.A3	Poetry
.A5	Drama
.A8	Prose. Prose fiction
	English
.E1	General
.E3	Poetry
.E5	Drama
.E8	Prose. Prose fiction
.F1–8	French 1/
.G1–8	German 1/
.I1–8	Italian 1/
.R1–8	Russian 1/
.S1–8	Spanish 1/
(2)	Other languages, A–Z

1/
Subarranged like .E1–8

INDIVIDUAL AUTHORS OR WORKS

TABLES OF SUBDIVISIONS

Authors with forty-nine numbers	XXXI	
Collected works		
Original editions and reprints. By date	0 or	50
To 1500: A00-A99		
1500-1599: B00-B99		
1600-1699: C00-C99		
1700-1799: D00-D99		
1800-1899: E00-E99		
1900-1999: F00-F99		
Editions with commentary, etc. By editor, A-Z	1	51
Selected works	2	52
Subarranged by editor, if given, or date		
Selections. Anthologies. Extracts	3	53
Subarranged by editor, if given, or date		
Translations. By language, A-Z	4	54
Subarranged by translator, if given, or date		
Separate works. By title	5-22	55-72
Only the more important have a special number or numbers assigned to them; the lesser works are to have Cutter numbers		
For subdivisions where one number is assigned to a work use Table XLI. For Cutter numbers, see Table XLIII		
Doubtful, spurious works (Collections only)	23	73
Imitations. Adaptations. Parodies (Collections only)	24	74
Relation to the drama and the stage. Dramatization	25	75
Translations (Comparative studies, etc.)	26	76
Illustrations (Portfolios, etc. without text, illustrations with quotations), see N8215, or the special artists in NC - NE as the case may be		
Class illustrated editions with other editions		
Class portraits, etc. of the author with his biography		
Biography, criticism, etc.		
Periodicals. Societies. Serials	29	79
Dictionaries, indexes, etc.	30	80
Class here general encyclopedic dictionaries only		
For special dictionaries, see the subject, e. g. 39, 89, Characters; 45, 95, Concordances and dictionaries		
Historical sources and documents of the biography or authors	.5	.5
For sources of literary works, see 36, 86		

INDIVIDUAL AUTHORS OR WORKS

TABLES OF SUBDIVISIONS

Authors with forty-nine numbers	XXXI		
Biography, criticism, etc. - Continued			
Autobiographical works			
Autobiography. By date	31.A2	or	81.A2
Journals. Memoirs. By title	.A3-39		.A3-39
Letters (Collections). By date	.A4		.A4
Letters to and from particular individuals.			
By correspondent (alphabetically)	.A41-49		.A41-49
General works	.A5-Z		.A5-Z
Early life. Education			
Love and marriage. Relation to women	} 32		82
Later life			
Relations to contemporaries. Times, etc. ...	33		83
Homes and haunts. Local associations.			
Landmarks	34		84
Anniversaries. Celebrations			
Memorial addresses			
Treatment in literature			
Iconography. Portraits. Monuments	} 35		85
Relics. Museums, exhibitions, etc.			
Authorship	36		86
Including manuscripts, sources, etc.			
For textual criticism, see 43, 93			
Chronology of works	37		87
Criticism and interpretation			
History			
General works	.3		.3
By region or country, A-Z	.4		.4
General works	38		88
Characters	39		89
Technique, plots, scenes, time, etc.	41		91
Treatment and knowledge of special			
subjects, A-Z	42		92
.A34 Aesthetics			
.A4 Allegory			
.A54 America			
.A66 Art			
.A7 Asia			
.B5 Bible			
.B58 Body, Human			
.B6 Books			
.C5 Ciphers			
.C7 Criticism (the author as critic)			
.D35 Death			
.D4 Devil			
.D56 Disguise			
.D6 Dogs			

INDIVIDUAL AUTHORS OR WORKS

TABLES OF SUBDIVISIONS

Authors with forty-nine numbers	XXXI

Criticism and interpretation
  Treatment and knowledge of special
     subjects, A–Z – Continued ....
	42 or 92

.D7 Dramatic works	
.D74 Dreams	
.E54 England	
.E5 Emotions	
.E8 Ethics	
.E9 Evil	
.F35 Fairy tales	
.F6 Folklore	
.F74 Freedom	
.G4 Geography	
.G43 Germany	
.G65 Greece	
.G7 Grotesque	
.G85 Guilt	
.H3 Happiness	
.H4 Heraldry	
.H5 History	
.H62 Humor. Satire Human body, see .B58	
.I82 Italy	
.L3 Law	
.L5 Literature	
.L6 Love	
.M3 Marriage	
.M37 Masques	
.M45 Memory	
.M95 Mysticism	
.M96 Myth	
.N2 Nature	
.O25 Occult	
.O5 Optimism	
.P3 Paradise	
.P5 Philosophy	
.P63 Poetic works	
.P64 Politics	
.P7 Prose	
.P8 Puritans	
.R4 Religion Satire, see .H62	

INDIVIDUAL AUTHORS OR WORKS

TABLES OF SUBDIVISIONS

Authors with forty-nine numbers	XXXI		
Criticism and interpretation 　Treatment and knowledge of special 　　subjects, A-Z - Continued	42	or	92
.S3　Science			
.S4　Semitic philology			
.S43　Senses and sensation			
.S47　Sex			
.S58　Social problems			
.S6　Socialism			
.S72　Stage history			
.S93　Suffering			
.T5　Time			
.W6　Women			
Textual criticism, commentaries, etc.	43		93
Language, style, etc.			
General works	44		94
Dictionaries.　Concordances	45		95
Grammar	46		96
Versification, meter, rhythm, etc.	47		97
Dialect, etc.	48		98

INDIVIDUAL AUTHORS OR WORKS

TABLES OF SUBDIVISIONS

Authors with nineteen or nine numbers	XXXII (19 nos.)	XXXIII (9 nos.)
Collected works		
By date	0	0
Use date letters as in Table XXXI		
By editor, if given	1	1
Selected works. Selections	2	2
Subarranged by editor, if given, or date		
Translations		
Modern versions of early authors in the		
same language. By translator, if given, or		
date	3	3.A2A-Z
Other. By language, A-Z	4	.A3-Z
Subarranged by translator, if given, or		
date		
Separate works. By title	5-10	4(A-Z)
Under each:		
XXXII, see Table XLI or XLIII		
XXXIII, see Table XLIII		
Apocryphal, spurious works, etc. (Collections		
only)	11	5
Illustrations, see N8215, or the special		
artists in NC - NE as the case may be		
Class illustrated editions with other		
editions		
Class portraits, etc., of the author with		
his biography		
Biography, criticism, etc.		
Periodicals. Societies. Serials	12.A1-5	6.A1-19
Dictionaries, indexes, etc.	.A6-Z	.A2-3
Autobiography, journals, memoirs. By title .	13.A3-39	.A31-39
Letters (Collections). By date	.A4	.A4
Letters to and from particular individuals.		
By correspondent (alphabetically)	.A41-49	.A41-49
General works	.A5-Z	.A5-Z
Criticism		
General works	14	7
Textual. Manuscripts, etc.	15	
Special		
Sources	16	
Other, A-Z	17	8
Including in Table XXXIII, language,		
grammar, style, etc.		
.A33 Adolescence		
.A35 Aesthetics		
.A6 Allegory		
.A63 Ambiguity		
.A75 Art		
.A89 Authority		

INDIVIDUAL AUTHORS OR WORKS

TABLES OF SUBDIVISIONS

Authors with nineteen or nine numbers	XXXII (19 nos.)	XXXIII (9 nos.)
Criticism		
Special		
Other, A-Z - Continued	17	8
.A9 Authorship		
.B52 Bible		
.B54 Biography (as a literary form)		
.B55 Biology		
.B6 Books and reading		
.B8 Burlesque (Literature)		
.C47 Characters and characteristics		
.C5 China		
.C56 The comic		
.C7 Creation		
.C8 Cuchulain		
.D53 Didactic literature		
.D7 Dramatic works		
.E25 Economics		
.E3 Education		
.E46 England		
.E8 Ethics		
.E9 Evil		
.F5 Fictional works		
.F55 Film adaptations		
.F64 Folklore		
.F7 French literature		
.G44 Geography		
.G47 Germany		
.H4 Heroes		
.H5 History		
Humor, see .S2		
.I33 Idealism		
.I4 Imagination		
.I44 Immortality		
.I46 Impressionism		
.I48 India		
.I5 Individualism		
.I52 Influence		
.I67 Ireland		
.I7 Irony		
.I8 Italy		
.K56 Kinship		
.L3 Landscape		
.L33 Language		
.L35 Laudatory poetry		
.L36 Law		

INDIVIDUAL AUTHORS OR WORKS

TABLES OF SUBDIVISIONS

Authors with nineteen or nine numbers	XXXII (19 nos.)	XXXIII (9 nos.)
Criticism		
Special		
Other, A-Z - Continued	17	8
.L5 Literature		
.L65 Love		
.L88 Luxury		
.M3 Marriage		
.M34 The marvelous		
.M4 Medicine		
.M47 Metamorphosis		
.M6 Money		
.M74 Music		
.M8 Mysticism		
.M82 Myth		
.M83 Mythology		
.O25 Occultism		
.P3 Parody		
.P4 Performing arts		
.P44 Pessimism		
.P5 Philosophy		
.P54 Plots		
.P58 Poetic works		
.P6 Political and social views		
.P67 Prose		
.P7 Prudence		
.P8 Psychology		
.P87 Puritanism		
.R3 Race problems		
Reading, see .B6		
.R37 Realism		
.R4 Religion		
.R47 Revenge		
.R5 Rivers		
.R6 Rogues and vagabonds		
.S2 Satire. Humor		
.S3 Scatology		
.S35 Science		
.S46 Settings		
Social views, see .P6		
.S6 Socialism		
.S7 Soldiers		
.S75 Stage history		

INDIVIDUAL AUTHORS OR WORKS

TABLES OF SUBDIVISIONS

Authors with nineteen or nine numbers	XXXII (19 nos.)	XXXIII (9 nos.)

Criticism
  Special
    Other, A-Z - Continued ....
	17	8

.S8 Style
    .S95 Symbolism
    .T4 Technique
    .T54 Time		

.T7 The tragic
    .T72 Tragicomedy
    .T73 Translations		

.V4 Versification
    .W37 War
    .W6 Women		

Language. Grammar. Style	18	

TABLE XXXIV
(5 nos.)

Single works with five numbers

0	Texts. By editor, if given, or date Including texts with commentaries
1	Selections. By editor, if given, or date Translations
2	Modern versions of early works in the same language. By translator, if given, or date
3	Other. By language, A-Z Subarranged by translator, if given, or date
4	Criticism

INDIVIDUAL AUTHORS OR WORKS

TABLES OF SUBDIVISIONS

Authors with four or five numbers	XXXV (5 nos.)	
Collected works		
To 1800. By date	0.A1 or	5.A1
1800-		
By date	.A2	.A2
By editor, if given	.A5A-Z	.A5A-Z
Translations. By language, A-Z	.A6-Z	.A6-Z
Subarranged by translator, if given, or date		
Selected works. Selections. By editor, if		
given, or date	1	6
Separate works. By title, A-Z (Table XLIII)	2	7
Biography, criticism, etc.		
Periodicals. Societies. Serials	3.A1-29	8.A1-29
Dictionaries, indexes, etc. By date	.A3	.A3
Autobiography, journals, memoirs. By title ...	.A4-43	.A4-43
Letters (Collections). By date	.A44	.A44
Letters to and from particular individuals.		
By correspondent (alphabetically)	.A45-49	.A45-49
General works	.A5-Z	.A5-Z
Criticism	4	9
Where only four numbers are provided, class		
Criticism with Biography		

TABLE XXXVI

Authors with two numbers

	Collected works
1.A1	By date
.A2A-Z	By editor, if given
.A3A-Z	Translations. By language, A-Z
.A4	Selected works. Selections. By date
.A5-Z	Separate works. By title
	Biography and criticism
2.A2	Dictionaries, indexes, etc. By date
.A3-39	Autobiography, journals, memoirs. By title
.A4	Letters (Collections). By date
.A41-49	Letters to and from particular individuals. By correspondent (alphabetically)
.A5-Z	General works

INDIVIDUAL AUTHORS OR WORKS

TABLES OF SUBDIVISIONS

Authors with one number or Cutter number	XXXVII	XXXVIII
Collected works		
By date	.A1	.x
By editor, if given	.A11-19	.xA11-19
Translations (Collected)		
Where the original language is English,		
French or German, omit numbers for		
original language		
English. By translator, if given, or date	.A2-29	.xA2-29
French. By translator, if given, or date	.A3-39	.xA3-39
German. By translator, if given, or date	.A4-49	.xA4-49
Other. by language	.A5-59	.xA5-59
Selected works. Selections. By date	.A6	.xA6
Separate works. By title	.A61-78	.xA61-78
Biography and criticism		
Dictionaries, indexes, etc. By date	.A79	.xA79
Autobiography, journals, memoirs. By title ...	.A8-829	.xA8-829
Letters (Collections). By date	.A83	.xA83
Letters to and from particular individuals.		
By correspondent (alphabetically)	.A84-849	.xA84-849
General works	.A85-Z	.xA85-Z

INDIVIDUAL AUTHORS OR WORKS

TABLES OF SUBDIVISIONS

Authors with one number or Cutter number	XXXIX (1 no.)	XL (Cutter no.)
Collected works		
By date	.A1	.x
By editor, if given	.A11-13	.xA11-13
Collected fiction. By date	.A15	.xA15
Collected essays. By date	.A16	.xA16
Collected poems. By date	.A17	.xA17
Collected plays. By date	.A19	.xA19
Translations (Collected)		
Where the original language is English, French or German, omit numbers for original language in A2-49		
Modern versions of early authors in the same language. By date	.A199	.xA199
English. By translator, if given, or date	.A2-29	.xA2-29
French. By translator, if given, or date	.A3-39	.xA3-39
German. By translator, if given, or date	.A4-49	.xA4-49
Other. By language	.A5-59	.xA5-59
Selected works. Selections. By date	.A6	.xA6
Separate works. By title	.A61-Z48	.xA61-Z458
Biography and criticism		
Dictionaries, indexes, etc. By date	.Z49	.xZ459
Autobiography, journals, memoirs. By title	.Z5A3-39	.xZ46-479
Letters (Collections). By date	.Z5A4	.xZ48
Letters to and from particular individuals. By correspondent (alphabetically)	.Z5A41-49	.xZ481-499
General works	.Z5A5-Z	.xZ5-999

INDIVIDUAL AUTHORS OR WORKS

TABLES OF SUBDIVISIONS

TABLE XLI

Separate works with one number

	Texts
.A1	By date
.A2A-Z	By editor, if given, A-Z
.A21-29	Modern versions of early works in the same language. By translator, if given, or date
.A3	Selections. By date
	Translations
	Where the original language is English, French or German omit numbers for original language
.A31-39	English. By translator, if given, or date
.A4-49	French. By translator, if given, or date
.A5-59	German. By translator, if given, or date
.A6-69	Other. By language
.A7-Z	Criticism

TABLE XLII

Authors or works with 3 successive Cutter numbers

(1)	date	Collected works. Selected works 1/
	A-Z	Separate works. By title, A-Z 1/
(2)		Translations. By language, A-Z
		Further subarranged by date
(3)	A-Z	Criticism

                       Note: In Table XLII, (1), (2), and (3) represent successive Cutter numbers, as, for example: .P4, .P5, .P6 .P6

1/
     For anonymous works or for authors with only one surviving work, the first number is used: (1) date, Texts. By date; (1)A-Z Texts. By editor, A-Z

INDIVIDUAL AUTHORS OR WORKS

TABLES OF SUBDIVISIONS

TABLE XLIII

Separate works with successive Cutter numbers

(1) date	Texts
A-Z	Translations. By language
	.A3-39 Modern versions of early works in same language. By translator, if given, or date
	.A4-Z Other languages, A-Z
(2)	Selections. By date
(3) A-Z	Criticism

Note: In Table XLIII, (1), (2), and (3) represent successive Cutter numbers, as, for example: .F6, .F7, .F8 or .F66, .F67, .F68

In the case of works where division (2) is inapplicable the numbers may be modified by using two Cutter numbers only, as .F4, .F5 or .F4, .F41

INDIVIDUAL AUTHORS OR WORKS

TABLES OF SUBDIVISIONS

TABLE XLIV

AUTHORS WITH TWO SUCCESSIVE CUTTER NUMBERS 1/

	Collected works
.x	By date
.xA11-13	By editor, if given
.xA15	Collected fiction. By date
.xA16	Collected essays. By date
.xA17	Collected poems. By date
.xA19	Collected plays. By date
	Translations (Collected)
	Where the original language is English, French or German, omit numbers for original language
.xA2-29	English. By translator, if given, or date
.xA3-39	French. By translator, if given, or date
.xA4-49	German. By translator, if given, or date
.xA5-59	Other. By language
.xA6	Selections. By date
.xA61-Z	Separate works. By title
	Biography and criticism
.x2A1-19	Periodicals. Societies. Serials
.x2A2	Dictionaries, indexes, etc. By date
.x2A31-39	Autobiography, journals, memoirs. By title
.x2A4	Letters (Collections.) By date
.x2A41-49	Letters to and from particular individuals. By correspondent (alphabetically)
.x2A5-Z	General works

1/

    .x=First Cutter number; .x2=second Cutter number. Replace .x or .x2 in table
with successive Cutter numbers for author, e. g. .B6, .B62 or .K57, .K572